Let Every Mother Rejoice

Rejoice

Kathy Collard Miller

ACCENT PUBLICATIONS
Colorado Springs, Colorado

Accent Publications
P.O. Box 36640
4050 Lee Vance View
Colorado Springs, Colorado 80936

Library of Congress Catalog Card Number 96-83163
ISBN 0-89636-325-2

Contents

Daughters of the King Bible Study Series

"So shall the king greatly desire thy beauty: for he is thy Lord; and worship thou him....The king's daughter is all glorious within: her clothing is of wrought gold."

Psalm 45:11,13

I'm Glad I'm a Mother

"**H**er children arise up, and call her blessed." Whether the world knows it or not, Proverbs 31:28 declares your role to be special, highly valued by God. Do you view your mothering role as a significant contribution to His plan for families and for eternity? You should—and take time to enjoy the privilege He has given you!

1. What do you like best about being a mother? Why?

What do you like least? Why?

2. In what ways does society encourage and discourage mothers?

Encourage   *Discourage*

Read Luke 1:46-56.

3. How would you summarize Mary's feelings in her song?

What is Mary's reaction to the news that she is pregnant?

Why was this pregnant, unwed teenager so happy?

How does Mary characterize God in her song?

Do you relate to Mary in any way as she expresses herself in her song? Explain.

How does focusing on God and His qualities/activities encourage you to rejoice in the experiences of motherhood?

4. God gave Elizabeth and Zacharias a child in their old age. He gave Mary the privilege of being the mother of His only begotten Son. As we look at the special births God recorded in Scripture for us, we see that He had a special plan for each family and each child. In what ways have you seen God's special plan fulfilled in your life through the birth and lives of your child(ren)?

What brings you joy as you remember your pregnancy and the birth of each child?

What brings you joy as you think about the personality, talents, and abilities of your child(ren)?

What brings you joy as you think about your child(ren)'s victories?

What brings you joy as you think about your child(ren)'s struggles?

Have you praised God for these joys? Write a short paragraph of prayer praising God for your child mentioning specific praises. If you need more space, use separate sheets of paper to write a paragraph for each child.

How do the truths of Psalm 139:13-16 relate to these joys?

5. What amazing things happened as a result of Jesus' birth as narrated in the following verses of Luke 2?

• 8-20 —

What comparable blessing did you receive as a result of your child's/children's birth(s)?

• 21-35 —

What comparable activities accompanied your child's/children's birth(s)?

• 36-38 —

Who else rejoiced with you at your child's/children's birth?

• 39-40 —

What joys do you see in the way your child(ren) is growing?

• 41-52 —

What was Mary's perspective during this time (2:19, 51)?

How do the memories of your good times as a mother help you regain a positive perspective when the challenges of mothering threaten your joy?

6. How do Luke 2:40 and 2:52 express the desire(s) of your heart for your child(ren)? Write your own prayer to God expressing those desires.

7. Read John 19:17-30. How do you think Mary may have felt when Jesus provided for her future (verses 25-27)?

How does the fact that Mary had other children (Mark 6:3) who could have taken care of her make Jesus' concern touching?

What events from Jesus' conception and birth that she had "treasured and pondered in her heart" (Luke 2:19, 51) might have brought her joy during this difficult time?

What events in your child's/children's life bring you joy during difficult times?

8. When our children face difficulties and challenges or suffer the pain in succumbing to temptations, we sometimes lose sight of the joys of motherhood. Yet God uniquely designed each of our children for a special purpose. If that purpose includes things that bring us sadness or discomfort, how can Mary's example strengthen us?

Remembering Mary's attitude from Luke 1:38, is there any way you need to change your attitude regarding the child(ren) God has given you?

9. Read Acts 1:1-14. Mary has suffered the most agonizing event a mother can experience – the death by torture of her child. Review Mary's song of praise in Luke 1:46-55. Do you think she remembered this exultation now? Do you think she still knew the joy of that day? How do you think Mary felt at this time? Explain your answers.

10. How could the following verses help you to remember the joys of motherhood when you become discouraged?

- Proverbs 3:5-6 —

- Isaiah 25:1 —

- Isaiah 26:3-4 —

- Jeremiah 29:11 —

- Ephesians 2:10 —

- Philippians 1:6 —

Which of those is most meaningful right now?

Memorize it and review it every day this week.

1. List the name of each of your children. Then write one thing about his personality or character that brings you joy. (Concentrate on who he is, not things he/she has done. Remember, happiness is not the same as joy.)

My Precious Princess and Daughter,

I designed the idea of mothers; I formed your heart to model mine. I created and crafted the honored role you have. I made you a mother! Rejoice!

Nourish the children I give you. Don't destroy these moments because of what I have not given to you. Let each child know your joy because they are part of your life. You are fulfilling My very special plan for you as you do. Just as I singled out Mary to have the special distinction of being My Son Jesus' mother, I have just as carefully and purposefully chosen you as the mother of your children. Rejoice!

Your children are some of My most precious gifts to you. Each is an eternal soul. And I have entrusted you with that life—to cherish, to guide, to introduce to Me. Don't let that responsibility overwhelm you. Rejoice in it!

I know there are times when the joys of motherhood seem to evaporate in the heat of the challenges your child gives you. But rejoice as these moments draw you closer to Me and transform you into the image of My Son, Jesus. Whether your child is compliant or strong-willed, I didn't make a mistake in giving you that child. I know exactly the plan I have for you and your family. Rejoice in Me!

Treasure your time with your beloved child. Your earthly life goes by so quickly, as I designed it to, so that you would value and cherish it. Look for the positives and ponder your child's unique design. I formed him or her in your womb. I know your child more intimately than you do. Hear My voice cheering you on, applauding your *work, your role as a mother. Trust Me and rejoice...in Me, in your child, in our walk together. You're doing a good job, My daughter.*

Lovingly,
Your Heavenly Father, the King

God Is My Parent

ow we'd love to be the perfect parent that God is to us! To be able to have such wisdom and insight would be fantastic! We would never respond inappropriately to our children. We would always have the right answers. Our patience would never run out. It can't happen, but let's take a look at our heavenly Father's parenting skills. We can learn from God's example.

1. What do you consider the key areas of parenting?

How have you seen God "parent" you in these areas?

When you think about God as your parent, what feelings or thoughts do you have toward Him?

2. Read Genesis 2. What did God provide for mankind in the following verses?

• 8-9 —

- 10-14 —

- 15 —

- 16-17 —

- 18-19 —

- 20-23 —

- 24-25 —

What do you think was God's motivation in providing all of this?

Do you think He benefited in any way from it? If so, in what way(s)?

Why do you think it was necessary for God to provide the challenge of temptation (verses 16-17)?

3. Read Genesis 3. How did Satan try to characterize God as a "bad" parent (verses 1-5).?

How did Eve's belief in that incorrect characterization encourage her disobedience (verses 1-7)?

As indicated in Eve and Adam's behavior in the following verses, what changed in their attitude toward their Father God?

• 6 —

• 7 —

• 8-10 —

• 12 —

• 13 —

Relate one or more of these to an attitude or action you may have seen in your child(ren)'s life.

After all Adam and Eve had been given, why do you think they would suddenly throw out all evidence to the contrary and believe these lies?

Why do you think your children misbehave or believe "lies" about you and your motives?

How did God deal with this change in His creation's view of Himself?

What is your usual way of dealing with these types of attitudes in your child(ren)?

How would you like to change your reactions in the future?

4. Do you think there is any connection between a mother's view of God and her responses as a mother? Explain.

5. Read Hebrews 12:5-11. How do these principles about discipline fit God's reactions toward Eve and Adam?

Based on the information given in Hebrews 12:5-11, what do you think are God's motives and intentions for you when disciplined by God?

In what ways is God a good example for mothers when they need to discipline their children?

As a mother, what underlying principles guide your discipline?

How can your discipline become more like God's example as expressed in Hebrews 12:5-11?

6. Read Psalm 103. How do the following verses describe God's relationship with you as His child?

- 2-5 —

- 6-7 —

- 8-9 —

- 10-12 —

- 13-14 —

• 15-18 —

Which of those verses is most meaningful to you?

What should be your response to such a wonderful heavenly
Father (verses 1,22)? How will you express this?

7. From the following verses, describe aspects of God's
Fatherhood. With each one, describe how a mother might
also behave in the same way. If possible, include a situation
when you had to respond to your child(ren) with those traits.

Verse(s)	God's Principles of Fatherhood	A Mother's Behavior & Situation
Psalm 89:30-34		
Psalm 147:3-6		
Isaiah 40:28		
Isaiah 41:10		
Isaiah 43:4		
Isaiah 43:25		

II Corinthians
1:3-4

I John
1:9

I John
3:1

Which of those verses about God are most important to you?

Which mother's reaction would you like to work on this week?

8. God's attributes also give us an example to follow. Identify one of God's attributes in each of the following verses and then pick one corresponding fruit from the nine fruit of the Spirit listed in Galatians 5:22-23. In the last column, evaluate your mothering reactions in that area and describe how you might grow through greater dependence upon the Holy Spirit.

Verse(s)	God's Attribute/ Fruit of the Spirit	Evaluation
Zephaniah 3:17		
Exodus 32:14		
John 3:16		

Matthew
11:29

Isaiah
25:1

Psalm
25:8

II Thessalonians
3:16

Psalm
86:15

Romans
11:22

What other attributes of God do you appreciate that are a good foundation for your role as a mother?

9. In the next week, think about how God parents you. As you act and react to your children, think about corresponding ways you act toward Him. How does He act? Keep a record of the characteristic or response of God you used as an example or foundation for your actions or words.

My Precious Princess and Daughter,

Remember how our relationship first began? Remember the ways you turned to Me and called Me Father? Can you hear Me claiming you as My child? That is why I love you so very much. My love for you is never-ending and unconditional.

I know you cannot be a perfect mother to the children I've given you. Don't worry. Remember that I do not want you to meet all of your child's needs. He would never learn to come to Me if you could.

You need to be needy, too, so that you will be dependent upon Me. You are weak, but remember that My strength is made perfect in your weakness. I would much rather you know Me intimately and draw from My strength rather than yours. Wouldn't you?

Precious one, let Me parent you, and as we grow closer together, you will discover that you are copying My parenting principles in the lives of the children I have entrusted to you. Grow in My grace, yet realize I am the only perfect parent. Look to Me when you doubt your way. Seek My wisdom.

Yes, your child will explore the boundaries you set. But you must be as firm in yours as I am in Mine. Your child will test your patience—and fill your life with joy—just as you do to Me. Only My patience has no end. Learn from Me, My child. Come to Me with all your problems, questions, and joys. Let Me share all of your life, My child. You are My daughter. I understand what you are going through.

Lovingly,
Your Heavenly Father, the King

Jesus Is My Encourager

D o you encourage your children? As mothers, one of our roles is to be the chief encourager of our children. We want to steer them toward godly actions and healthy attitudes—through our own. We have an example to follow—our Lord Jesus Christ. His heart of encouragement showed in His interactions with His disciples, with strangers, even with those who would be His enemies. He offers the same encouragement to us, so we can be that kind of encourager to our children.

1. What do you like best about your mothering role as an encourager and motivator?

When is it most difficult to be encouraging?

2. From the following passages in Matthew, identify the action or feelings of those encountering Jesus and His reaction/ attitudes to them.

Verse(s)	People's Action/ Feelings	Jesus' Reaction/ Attitude
8:18-22		
8:23-27		
9:20-22		
10:1		
15:32-37		
19:16-22		

What principles of encouragement can a mother learn from Jesus' example?

Which of Jesus' reactions do you need most as you respond to your child(ren)?

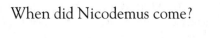

Read John 3:2.

When did Nicodemus come?

What did he want?

Were these simple questions or did they take time? What principles can you draw from this which would be appropriate mothering responses?

How did Jesus encourage Nicodemus?

3. *Read John 4:1-42.*

Jesus was exhausted (verse 6), a state most mothers (especially of infants or young children) can relate to. When a mother feels that way, how might she be tempted to respond?

Yet, how did He respond?

4. As we motivate our children, we may be tempted at times to just tell them what to do or believe instead of encouraging their mental or spiritual growth. What purpose do you think was fulfilled through Jesus posing a series of questions or challenges?

How do Jesus' reactions encourage a mother not to be intolerant of a child expressing doubts about his/her faith?

5. Why do you think Jesus was patient with this round-about conversation?

6. Why do you think some mothers are impatient with children who want to talk about their spiritual doubts or questions, or even act them out in rebellion?

Have you ever responded impatiently to such questioning or behavior? If so, how would you respond the next time in a similar situation?

7. There comes a time when a challenge to faith or a confrontation of sin is necessary. How are Jesus' actions an encouragement for mothers at times like that?

8. Jesus' interaction brings good results (verses 39-42). Have you ever experienced the same kind of satisfaction in encouraging spiritual growth in your child(ren)? What happened?

9. Read John 5:19 and 30. Why was Jesus able to do so much?

What does that indicate should be our source of strength or wisdom?

What promise can you claim in James 1:5 to encourage you as you respond to your children?

10. What encouragement does God offer to you if your children don't always act the way you want them to?

- II Corinthians 1:3-4 —

- I Thessalonians 5:16-18 —

- James 1:2-4 —

11. Most of us regard Jesus as Someone who was always there to meet everyone's needs, and mothers certainly expect the same from themselves. Yet what does Matthew 14:23 and Luke 5:15-16 indicate is necessary?

Is spending time with God your priority? Why do mothers need to follow this example?

12. We cannot receive encouragement from Jesus unless we spend time with Him. How would you characterize your walk with God in these spiritual disciplines?

- prayer —

• Bible study —

• fellowship with other Christians —

• Scripture memorization —

If you are saying to yourself that you don't have time for these, do you need to re-examine your priorities? What can you do to put time with God first so you can be more of what you want to be for your children?

13. When you think of Jesus as an encourager and motivator, what stands out to you about His example?

As a result of His example, what will you do differently this week as you interact with your children? Think of specific things or attitudes you will do or show this week to encourage each child.

My Precious Princess and Daughter,

Do you feel Me cheering for you? Can you see in My Word that I believe in you? Let Me be your encourager.

I know how much you need to lean back and trust Me. Yet the world and the demands of your children try to pull you away. Don't let them. Stay close to Me.

You will feel My arms around you when the difficulties of motherhood drive you to tears. You will feel My hand wipe away those tears and soothe your anguished heart. You will feel my joy well up inside you as you look for ways to encourage your child—and see him respond.

Remember, the world is trying to tear your child down, too. Let him know that there is one place in all the world where he can go where someone is always on his side. Let him know beyond any doubt that that person and that place is you. That is what makes the difference.

I am standing with you. You can stand with your child. That doesn't mean you always approve of his actions. I don't always approve of yours. But there is always the certainty that you can come to Me and talk it out. You can always ask for My forgiveness. You can always count on the fact that even if I discipline you, I love you. That is what your child needs from you, too.

Daughter, I love you more than you can ever realize. I am always in your corner, encouraging you to do your best. Let your child feel your encouragement. Let your child see your confidence in Me.

Lovingly,
Your Heavenly Father, the King

Obstacles to My Good Mothering

Although many of us enter motherhood expecting only the joys, there are obstacles to joy lurking ahead in the dimness of time yet to come. Being aware of possible difficulties and trusting God will enable us to sidestep them as much as possible.

1. How do you define a "good" mother?

What obstacles to "good" mothering have you encountered?

2. Read Genesis 25:19-34. Under what stressful circumstances did Rebekah become a mother?

verses 21-23 —

What seeds for obstacles were sown in this family's relationships?

verses 27-28 —

verses 29-34 —

Was there favoritism shown in your family as you grew up? If so, in what ways were you influenced by it?

3. Read Genesis 27:1-46. Parental favoritism is certainly a serious obstacle to loving family relationships. What could Rebekah have done constructively to try to influence Isaac?

What did Rebekah's favoritism create within her and her family according to verses 41-43.

What do Rebekah's actions tell us about her attitudes toward God? (Review God's promise in Genesis 25:23.)

Do any of your responses regarding your children reveal your attitudes about God, positive and/or negative?

4. Read Job 1:1—2:10. Use your imagination to describe the kind of life Job's wife had as a wife and mother (Job 1:1-5).

Look at the interaction between Satan and God (Job 1:6-12). If God and Satan were talking about you right now, would their conversation be different or the same? If different, how?

Along with Job, what did his wife experience in the following verses in Job 1?

14-15 —

16 —

17 —

18-19 —

Trauma after trauma overwhelmed her family. How did Job respond (Job 1:20-22)?

How did his wife respond (2:9)?

5. Although we do not know all the underlying causes for her response (but can sympathize with her deep grief), what obstacles to good mothering might each of the following wrong ideas have contributed to her reaction?

"My children are the most important things in my life."

"My children didn't deserve to die."

"God is a good God only when He makes good things happen."

Do you see any of these attitudes (or other, similar ones) in your thinking? Explain.

What truths do the following verses reveal that would help in such difficult times?

• Psalm 18:30 —

• Psalm 138:8 —

• Isaiah 25:1 —

• Isaiah 43:1b-5 —

• Romans 8:28 —

• II Corinthians 12:9 —

Which of those verses is most meaningful to you? Why?

7. From a child's point of view, good mothering might entail what?

As much as you might want to, you cannot fulfill your child's every desire. Why would it be wrong to do so?

8. What kinds of obstacles to good mothering do you think the following would create? Think of the result or consequences in the child or the relationship between child and parent.

Anger —

Impatience —

Lack of respect to the child —

Lack of respect to your spouse —

Covetousness/materialism —

Pride —

Critical attitude toward others —

Lying —

What can you do to avoid these obstacles? Find a Scripture verse that counters each of these.

9. Mothers usually try to protect their children from all of life's unhappy circumstances and often become over-controlling. Describe how such a goal could be destructive in a mother's life.

How could it be destructive to a child's life?

How would you describe a good balance between trying to legitimately protect or control a child while allowing him/her to learn from difficult situations?

God has given you the responsibility to protect your child whenever possible. Name some dangers that a mother should protect a child from and which she actually has the control to do so.

Name some difficulties a mother can't protect her child from but must trust God will use in her child's life?

10. In what ways have you seen difficult situations correct or purify your child?

11. Ultimately, every spiritual decision is your child's. It is not something you can control. How should a mother respond to an erring child (II Timothy 2:25-26)?

12. Is it possible to throw obstacles to spiritual growth in your child's way? What and how might that happen?

What have you found valuable in finding a balance in this area?

13. As you review this lesson, what changes do you want to make in your mothering as a result?

My Precious Princess and Daughter,

I understand why mothering can be difficult. The world is a frightening place because My enemy, Satan, doesn't want you to succeed in the one thing that matters most—showing your child how to find My Son Jesus as his Savior.

The obstacles to being the good mother you really long to be are many. Some of them spring from deep inside you. I want you to take a close look at that. What kinds of attitudes have you unleashed? Not setting boundaries for your children or not enforcing them is as harmful as having boundaries that are too strict. My love isn't a "do or have whatever you want" kind of love. Yours should not be either.

Rejoice when you become more aware of flaws in your thinking. I appreciate your sensitive, teachable heart. If you find a tendency to favor one child over the other, just remember that I gave all your children to you and uniquely designed each one to impact the world and you. I want you to make a choice to love each child equally. You may not always feel loving, but you can decide to be loving. Let Me be your example.

I don't expect you to be perfect, just continually growing. I've made your child more forgiving and resilient than you can imagine, so don't let my enemy, Satan, condemn you. With Me, there is always hope. I never give up working within you to make you more of the mother you want to be. Be confident in My power. You are important to me, daughter. There are no obstacles we cannot overcome together!

Lovingly,
Your Heavenly Father, the King

Sometimes I Get So Mad!

Kids can be frustrating! Cute and winsome one minute—testing the patience of Job the next. It's amazing how loving we feel one minute—and how angry we can feel the next. The testing of our patience may be good for us, but we all need skills for coping with the emotions that accompany child-engineered frustration.

1. What part of mothering frustrates you the most?

What behavior of your child challenges your patience most often?

2. Remember how Jesus said He was tempted in all points like we are? Jesus is our example because we can see how He responded in frustrating times. From the following passages, indicate the behavior of those Jesus dealt with and the way Jesus handled it.

Verse(s)	The People's Behavior	Jesus' Response
Mark 2:23-28		

Verse(s)	The People's Behavior	Jesus' Response
Mark 4:35-41		
Mark 6:1-6		
Mark 7:1-16		
Mark 8:10-21		
Mark 14:32-42		
Mark 14:43-49		

Now note how that situation could apply to mothering.

Situation	Application of Jesus' Response

3. What are the characteristics of God's anger?

• Exodus 22:22-24 —

• Nehemiah 9:16-17 —

• Psalm 30:5 —

• Isaiah 54:8 —

What do the characteristics of God's anger say to you about yours?

4. Read John 2:13-17; Ephesians 4:26, and Hebrews 4:15. Jesus felt anger. Yet He did not sin. He knows we feel anger, and commands us not to sin. So what can we conclude about some kinds of anger?

What do you do when the first flash feelings of anger rise within you?

Have you ever noticed the warning signals your body gives you about those first flash feelings? Check any of the following reactions that you've sensed at those times:

__ tense muscles   __ clenched jaw

__ tightened fist   __ voice rising

__ withdrawing/becoming quiet   __ feeling cold or hot.

__ having more energy

How could recognizing those warning signals of your first flash of angry feelings help you cope with your anger when it is caused by or directed toward your children?

Anger creates energy. It is often helpful to dissipate that energy by doing something physical like jogging in place, pounding a pillow, taking a walk, or calling a friend. What kind of physical activity will you do to release the energy rather than let it engulf your children?

5. A possible source of anger for a mother is when she and her husband don't agree on the way they should discipline their children. Have you experienced this? If so, explain the differing viewpoints. If not, explain how you and your husband reached an agreement on discipline.

What do you think is the solution when you don't agree about appropriate discipline?

How could a wise woman "build her house" when facing that situation (Proverbs 14:1)?

How do you think she might foolishly "tear it down"?

6. Some mothers incorrectly think anger is a disciplinary tool, as if their anger should motivate their child to obey. But what is the truth?

• Proverbs 15:1 —

• Proverbs 25:11,15 —

• Ephesians 6:4 —

7. Another source of parental anger is believing we can control our child when actually he is responsible for his own decisions. A mother is certainly responsible to train him as well as she can, but she can't guarantee he'll make godly choices. Read Ezekiel 18:1-13, 20. Summarize in your own words the principle stated there.

If a mother doesn't understand the principle expressed in that passage, and thinks her child is a reflection of her, how would that increase her anger?

8. What advice do the following verses from Proverbs give about anger and how would you apply each verse to mothering?

<u>**Principle**</u>   <u>**Application**</u>

14:29

15:18

16:32

46

Principle	_Application_
17:14	
19:11	
29:11	
29:22	

How can you apply these principles in your mothering?

9. Read Ephesians 4:15a, 25-32. How might anger keep a mother from "speaking the truth in love" with her family (15a, 25)?

Based on verse 26, it is possible for anger to not always be sinful. When might a mother's anger be appropriate?

What would be an example of sinful anger?

How do you think the devil might use a mother's anger as an opportunity for evil (verse 27)?

Once you start to feel angry, what have you found helpful to keep unwholesome words from devastating one of your children (verse 29)?

What is the most important principle for dealing with our anger (verse 32)?

How does forgiveness diminish anger?

Describe, if possible, a recent experience when your choice to forgive diminished your anger as a mother.

According to verse 32, why should we forgive others?

10. When we grieve the Holy Spirit with our anger (verses 30-31), how can we restore our fellowship with God (I John 1:9)?

Many moms have trouble forgiving themselves and accepting God's forgiveness when they overreact toward their children. Identify from these verses the characteristics of God's forgiveness.

• Nehemiah 9:16-17 —

• Psalm 86:5 —

• Isaiah 55:7 —

Which characteristic do you need to focus on the most today?

How will that characteristic help you to forgive yourself and accept God's forgiveness?

11. Besides the benefits of forgiveness for us, why else does God want to forgive us (Isaiah 43:25)?

12. When we feel condemned and accused before God, who should we recognize as the source of that (Revelation 12:10)?

Are we ever condemned by God as Christians (Romans 8:1)?

God does convict us, but He never condemns us. What do you think are the differences between the two?

13. If we do fear that we've harmed our children in some way with our anger, what comfort do the principles of God's promises in these verses provide?

• Isaiah 43:18-19 —

• Jeremiah 29:11 —

• Joel 2:25-26 —

14. When you begin to feel angry, what will you do to diminish that feeling and allow God to control it?

For the next week, record the causes of your anger in your mothering role. (Remember, causes of anger often involve pride, need for control, fear, righteous anger over a wrong act, etc.) Think about how you can apply this lesson's insights to the situations.

Situation	_Cause of Anger_	_My Response_

My Precious Princess and Daughter,

Life can be frustrating, can't it? I'm sure there are times when you'd just rather resign from mothering. I understand. My Son, Jesus, sometimes felt frustrated with the people who surrounded Him, too. He wanted everyone to believe in Him, but so many refused. You want your child to obey you for his own good. And it's frustrating when he won't do what you say! (Remember, I'm your Father. I know all about My children not doing what I say.)

As you struggle in this, remember that it's what you do with anger that makes it right or wrong and constructive or destructive. My Son, Jesus, was angry and yet He never sinned. You can feel angry and yet not grieve My Spirit. But take care of it quickly for My enemy, Satan, is looking for any little opportunity to make you sin and feel defeated. And anger is a wide open door to sin.

Be encouraged, My beloved, for I have conquered our enemy and Jesus is interceding for you right now at My right hand. My longsuffering and forgiveness are yours as soon as you ask. Immediately! I love you so much, I don't want any sin to separate us, My precious one. Not even for a second. I know exactly how I'm going to strengthen you and help you respond.

Talk to Me about your anger; know that I'll never leave you or forsake you; you can never turn My love "off." Together we can face any situation, any frustration—and I'll never give up on you. I love you too much.

Lovingly,
Your Heavenly Father, the King

Choosing to Act in Love

L *ove! That's what being a mother is all about. We mothers have very loving hearts. We would willing bear our children's pain, protect them from hurts, open the doors to advantages we'll never know. Yet, even with all that love, we still don't have a perfect relationship with our children. Love can't guarantee a smooth, problem-free family life, but the more we learn about how to express it, the more we will be able to love—with God's kind of love.*

1. How much did you or do you count on your love for your child to create a good relationship between you?

In what ways in your mothering role do you think you love well and in what ways do you think your love is weak?

2. Read Exodus 2:1-10. How did Jochebed, Moses' mother, show love for her new son? (See verses 2-3, 9-10 especially.)

What did she risk by protecting him? (Also see Exodus 1:15-22.)

Have you ever had to protect your child at the risk of being criticized by others?

3. Sometimes our love for our children makes us act a little foolish. Read Matthew 20:20-28. How did that apply to Salome, the mother of James and John?

What was admirable, yet misdirected, about her desires?

How did her request show her beliefs about Jesus?

What trouble did her interference bring her sons (verse 24)?

Does Jesus' response to Salome give you any comfort when you think of misdirected requests or desires you may have had for your child(ren)?

4. The Apostle Paul was like a parent to many of his spiritual children. From the following verses in I Thessalonians 2, identify how Paul expressed his love for them.

7 —

8 —

9 —

10 —

11-12 —

5. Even though Paul loved his "children," he knew he couldn't keep them from experiencing hardships. Instead, what do the following verses say about his attitude toward problems in life?

• II Corinthians 10:13 —

• I Thessalonians 3:3-4 —

• II Timothy 2:3 —

Have you ever tried to protect your child(ren) but he/she didn't appreciate it? Explain.

Would you do anything different the next time a similar situation arises?

6. Look at II Peter 1:4-8. What elements create the foundation for growing as a loving mother?

Which ones do you need to add more of?

Why would these qualities make you a more loving mother?

7. Now read I Corinthians 13. Give an example which demonstrates each of the following traits of love as they relate to a mother's love.

is patient —

is kind —

not envious —

does not boast —

isn't proud —

isn't rude —

isn't self seeking —

not easily angered —

keeps no record of wrongs —

doesn't delight in evil —

rejoices with truth —

it protects —

it trusts —

it hopes —

it perseveres —

8. What three things can children be expected to do (verse 11)?

Describe how your child(ren) have done those three things.

Situation	*Adult Perspective*	*Child's Perspective*
1.		
2.		
3.		

Mothers can easily forget that children will act like children and as a result become exasperated with them. When did you recently allow unrealistic expectations of your child's behavior to affect the way you expressed your mother's heart of love?

The next time a similar situation occurs, what will you do instead?

9. In what ways have you seen your child develop in his ability to "know fully" (verse 12) as he/she has matured?

How does that give you hope and expectations for the future?

10. As you think about being a loving mother, what qualities do you see as most important?

How will you demonstrate these to your child(ren) this week?

My Precious Princess and Daughter,

I see your heart. I know the love you have for the children I have given you. You are a good mom. But remember, My beloved one, love is not just a feeling, it is a choice. You may not always feel loving toward your child, but you can choose to act in loving ways.

That includes understanding that your child is going to act like a child. He is immature. He thinks like a child. In time, he will grow and mature, but please don't expect him to be an adult. Remember my patience with you as you sometimes act spiritually immature. You are progressing in maturity and so will your precious child.

In order for you both to grow, I must allow trials in your lives. If that makes Me seem less than good, just remember that My nature never changes. I am also working to bring My agape qualities to full fruit in your life. That will make you an even more loving mom.

I know your heart. Will you trust Mine? The fierce love inside you toward your children is good, natural, a reflection of Mine for you. Rejoice in that. You would willingly die in place of your children. And that is what I, in My Son Jesus, did for you. I know all about being a loving Parent.

I won't allow anything in your lives except what I intend to use for good. I love you and your family with an everlasting love.

Lovingly,
Your Heavenly Father, the King

My Kids, My Home—My Stress

H ow do we get it all done? With only 24 hours in a day, we must be chauffeur, maid, cook, housekeeper, sometimes nurse, often a breadwinner, usually the peacekeeper and diplomat, possibly the home repair person, financier, wife, listening ear, and mom. We want the best for our families and that includes making home a pleasant environment for them. We'd like to be all things to all people—family and friends. Sometimes the stress that creates threatens to overwhelm us. How wonderful it is that God has reasonable expectations of us.

1. What distinctions do you see between the roles of mothering and homemaking?

Do you consider yourself balanced in your roles between mothering and homemaking? If not, how are you unbalanced?

If you work outside the home, what is the most difficult aspect for you of being a mother while working?

2. Read verse 11. List as many reasons as you can for why a husband's heart would trust in his wife.

Is there an area where you wonder if your husband can trust in you? If so, what do you need to do about it?

3. List the many ways you do your husband good (verse 12). Then list ways you may have done him "evil."

I have done good for my husband by…

I have done "evil" for my husband by…

In what way could you improve your goodness to your husband?

4. Do you delight in your ability to provide for your family or are you waiting until something is done perfectly before you delight in it (verse 13)?

5. Looking at verses 14 through 21, what attitudes about her activities do you think motivate this woman?

How does she give quality care to her family and others?

Identify modern activities that might be synonymous to what she did.

Verse	Kind of Care	Modern Activities
14		
15		
16		
17		
18		
19		
20		
21		

How would these motives and attitudes relieve the stresses of homemaking?

6. Based on verses 22 through 25, how would you describe her physical appearance and bearing?

7. How does she relate to others in her home and outside it (verse 26)?

8. Verse 27 seems to be a summary about this woman's homemaking philosophy. Write here your own summary about her.

Summarize your own homemaking philosophy as a paraphrase of this verse.

9. What results does she enjoy (verses 28-29)?

What results do you want to achieve? What do you want your children (and husband) to say about you?

10. What two things does this woman refuse to depend upon and what does she depend on instead (verse 30)?

Is there anything besides God that you are trusting in to try to make your life a success and get the praise you need?

What helps this woman resist seeking praise for herself (verses 30-31)?

What should a Christian woman boast about (Galatians 6:14 and Romans 15:17-18)?

What difference does that make in someone's life?

Have you seen it make a difference in your life?

11. This woman is described as strong several times. What area described in her life would you like to grow stronger in?

12. What impresses you most about this woman?

13. The record of the Proverbs 31 Woman is undoubtedly the fruit from the span of her adult years rather than one season of her life. She can be an inspiration to us, but what would God not want us to do, based on Galatians 6:4?

How have you seen it create stress in you as you look at other women's lives around you?

What do you think God wants your attitude to be?

How will you prevent the stress of comparing your homemaking management to others' from happening in the future?

14. *Read Luke 10:38-42.*
Do you relate more to Mary or to Martha?

What aspects of homemaking make you feel worried and upset the most?

What do you think God wants you to do about the stresses of homemaking?

What was wrong with Martha's priorities?

How is Mary an example for you?

How would making a consistent devotional life your priority over everything else relieve the stresses of homemaking and mothering?

What can you do to make that happen more often?

It's true. Children and household management do cause stress. But just as Jesus wanted Mary and Martha to concentrate on Him, we mothers need to remember that our children won't always be young and underfoot. Do you find that housework seems to be more urgent than giving attention to your children? If so, why?

Have you found any keys to making quality time with your children a priority?

15. List the major stresses you sense in your life. Then list one thing you will do about it either to relieve the stress or manage the stress.

Things That Cause Me Stress	*What I Will Do About It*

My Precious Princess and Daughter,

My child, I know your desire is to make a loving home for your family. Don't be discouraged by all the details that your human world creates and says you must do. Your child loves you whether or not your house is perfect. You're the mother who fills his life with love, and your impact in his life is incredible.

Please stop judging your value on the neatness of your house. A floor will get dirty again. The dishes will always need to be cleaned. There will be unending laundry. You will never have a perfectly clean house—you have kids and they will mess it up! Relax amid the evidence that you have children, a home, a place to mess up.

That's not where your worth lies. Your worth is based in the fact that you are My child. My love for you never wavers because it's not determined by your performance or an uncluttered family room.

Take your eyes off that and let My unconditional love wrap you in a cocoon of confidence and acceptance. When My enemy, Satan, whispers in your heart that the house is a disaster and so are you, don't believe him. I love order and beauty. I created both. But you and your children are My priority. I would much rather see you concentrate on giving your children the attention they need. After all, they'll be going to heaven with you; the dust-bunnies under your bed won't.

My daughter, you are a delight to Me. Rest and delight in the children I've given you. You can have a perfectly spotless home when they are gone. And it will be filled with better memories.

Lovingly,
Your Heavenly Father, the King

Impacting My Child Now and for Eternity

*W*hat a privilege—and a responsibility! God has entrusted us *with the eternal souls of our children to nurture, to guide, to teach. The decision to accept Christ is theirs alone, but we are to show them how and why this is the most important decision they can ever make. Our mother's hearts want our children to develop an intimate relationship with God and reflect His characteristics in their lives. Although we may feel inadequate at times to encourage that to happen, we can trust God to work in their lives...and ours.*

1. In what ways have you created an environment where your children can grow spiritually?

In what ways have you not succeeded as well as you would like?

2. Read Matthew 15:21-28. What personal strength did this woman have on behalf of her child?

How did this demonstrate her faith?

What do you think about Jesus' delay in answering her (verse 23) and why do you think He did that?

Have you experienced any delays in God answering your prayers for your children or the prayers of your children?

How did that make you feel?

Did you see any purpose(s) eventually revealed through the delay?

This loving mother proved her faith in Jesus. How have you proved or demonstrated your faith to your children?

3. Some mothers featured in the Bible did not demonstrate a godly example for their children, like Jezebel. Read I Kings 18:13, 19:1-2, and 21:1-16. What kind of example did Jezebel give her children?

What kinds of lessons or behaviors would they learn from her actions?

Who was her son (I Kings 22:40)?

What kind of man was he (I Kings 22:51-52)?

Are there any negative behaviors or attitudes in your life which will affect your children? What can you or should you do to change?

4. Another poor example of mothering was Herodias. Read Mark 6:17-29. How did she influence her daughter?

How do you influence your children? Think of one act that may have influenced them for good and one act that may have influenced them for bad.

What qualities in your life do you think your children need to see so that your influence in more positive than negative?

5. In contrast to Jezebel and Herodias are the instructions for godly parents in Deuteronomy 6:4-7. According to verse 4, why should we teach our child(ren) about God?

What is required of us in order to teach them about Him (verse 5)?

What two methods does verse 7 seem to indicate are important and how would you define or differentiate them?

Verse 7 also suggests four specific opportunities for teaching. What are they and how have you used each one to teach your child?

Opportunity	**What you've done**
*	
*	
*	
*	

Which of those do you find easiest and which are most difficult to use?

Do you think it is possible to speak too often about God to your child(ren)?

Your life, not just your words, impacts the image your child forms of God. What else must accompany your talking (James 1:19)?

What do you think your "listening ear" communicates to your child?

If we talk but don't listen, what impression could that give to our children about God, whom we are supposed to be modeling?

6. What is the foundational attitude within us that will influence our children (II Timothy 1:5)?

How have you seen that element affect your child(ren)?

How would II Timothy 1:7 be God's encouragement to you as a mother?

Even though Lois and Eunice obviously provided a spiritually nurturing home, Timothy still needed to grow spiritually on his own. What do the following verses in II Timothy seem to indicate he struggled with?

1:7 —

1:8 —

2:1 —

2:15 —

2:16 —

2:22 —

2:23 —

Do you see any of those same struggles in your child(ren)?

How have you tried to help your child deal with that weakness from a spiritual standpoint?

7. Many mothers believe if they could somehow be perfect (or at least better), their children wouldn't have as many struggles. How do the previous ideas give a more realistic perspective (remembering that Timothy even had Paul as his mentor)?

What do the following verses communicate about the process of growth expected of all of us, especially children?

I Thessalonians 3:11—4:1 —

I Timothy 4:15 —

II Timothy 3:14-15 —

8. What are we promised as we pray for our children (James 5:16)?

What results are you currently trusting God for in your child(ren)'s life?

9. Praying the actual words of Scripture for our children is one of the most powerful things we can do. Why is that true (II Timothy 3:16-17; Hebrews 4:12)?

Read the following passages and then summarize them in your own words in the form of a prayer for each of your children; be sure to include their name(s).

Ephesians 1:18-20 —

Ephesians 3:14-21 —

Ephesians 6:10-17 —

Philippians 1:9-11 —

Philippians 4:6-8 —

Colossians 1:9-12 —

10. From the following passages, what other spiritual character traits should we pray for our children to develop?

Galatians 5:22-23 —

Colossians 3:12-15 —

I John 2:15 —

I John 3:18 —

James 1:5 —

James 1:20 —

What can you do to encourage the development of these qualities in your children?

Which of those qualities are most needed by your child(ren) right now? Write here a prayer regarding your desire for that.

Will you share these prayers with your child(ren) at least two days this week?

11. Read Hebrews 12:11-17. As we consistently train and discipline our children, what will they experience (verse 11)?

What character traits do you hope to see in your children that could be called "righteousness"?

When your children are feeling "feeble" and "weak" (verse 12) in choosing the right way, what do you think is the best way to respond?

As God works in their lives, what will His discipline help to grow in their lives (verses 13-15)?

Esau is an example of someone who lacked character strength. What do you think his choices demonstrate were his basic moral and spiritual motives? (See Genesis 25:27-34.)

Do you see any potential character weaknesses in your child(ren) that you could help them overcome? How?

What positive character traits do you see already in each of your children?

12. What will happen as our children grow in those areas?

I Peter 1:6-7 —

II Peter 1:8 —

How will you claim II Peter 1:12-13 in regard to the spiritual education of your children?

Since we cannot guarantee our child's response to God, so what should our attitude be (Isaiah 26:3-4)?

13. In what one, specific way will you try to have a greater spiritual impact upon your child(ren) in the next week?

My Precious Princess and Daughter,

I know you love Me. I see your desire to grow closer to Me. To know My heart. To be more like Me. And that pleases Me so much.

I know you sometimes feel ill-equipped to nurture your children and help them grow to see their need of Me and My Son Jesus. But every time you make going to church a priority, and take time to read My Word with your children, and ensure time during each day to pray with them, I am honored.

I designed your family exactly according to My plan. In fact, I designed the very idea of families so that the truth about Me would be shared and taught within a loving group that would remind you of the rest of My family. I have commissioned you to be My personal tutor to your children. Help them to know Me better.

At times it may not seem that your children are interested or learning anything, but don't worry. The final chapter of their lives hasn't been written yet. I am working.

As I do that, tell them often of your trust in Me. Stay alert for any opportunity. What may seem like the most common moment might be appropriate for sharing how I have worked in your life. And remember to be a good listener, because I am.

Those drops of spiritual water will create a deep thirst that will lead your child to a well of living water. Trust Me, faithful daughter. Remember My power is unlimited. Open your eyes and don't discount even the smallest thing I do. You can't see the big picture, but I can. And always remember that I love your child even more than you do.

Lovingly,
Your Heavenly Father, the King

Disciplining My Children

orrection. Discipline. No one enjoys being the one who enforces the rules, yet, it is necessary. God uses it in our lives to help us grow in our faith. He expects us as mothers to use it in order to see godly fruit produced in our children. This isn't always a simple or easy task, for it requires our confidence and consistency. Yet God can strengthen us to teach and to give them the correction they need.

1. How do you define "discipline" as it relates to responding to your children's disobedience?

What disciplining techniques have you found effective?

2. Many parents think of disciplining as just "correction," but there are actually three levels:
Instruction: verbally giving directions.
Teaching: being involved in the process of helping your child learn a correct behavior.
Correction: giving a consequence for disobedience once the child understands right and wrong in that area.

What similarities does that information have to the work God's Word does in our lives as expressed in II Timothy 3:16?

What does II Timothy 3:17 indicate will be the result in our lives (and in our children's also)?

Of the three levels listed above, which one(s) do you believe you do consistently?

If there are any that you need to work on, write your plan for doing that here.

3. Read Hebrews 12:5-11. What principles of discipline can you identify from the following verses?

5-6 —

7-8 —

9 —

10 —

11 —

How have you seen those principles used by God in your life?

Which verse gives you the most hope or encouragement for shaping your child(ren)'s future by effective discipline?

4. Why do you think our children (and we, too, when God disciplines us) have trouble believing the truth of Hebrews 12:5-6?

Why do you think getting disciplined would make a child feel like a part of the family (even though he may protest receiving it) (verse 8)?

5. When your child doesn't agree or approve of your efforts to discipline him, how do you feel?

Do you think parents should seek their children's agreement or approval for their disciplinary actions? Why or why not?

How do parents demonstrate that they are seeking or wanting their child's approval or agreement?

No one enjoys being disciplined, so you may never get agreement or approval for the discipline you feel is necessary. How can you seek and impart understanding of why the child is being disciplined?

6. Why is it difficult for parents to discipline consistently? Give as many reasons as you can think of.

Which of those do you succumb to the most?

Read I Samuel 2:12-36. Why was Eli negligent about disciplining his sons (verse 29)?

Write out what you would tell a mother who is struggling with the following causes of inconsistency.

I want my child's approval and acceptance.

If I discipline him, he won't want to be my friend. (He won't like me.)

I was abused when I was a child and I don't want to do the same thing to my child.

I have too many other things to do or think about.

If I discipline her, her creativity and spontaneity will be crushed.

I'm afraid my anger will get out of control.

I've tried some techniques before and they didn't work.

I don't have the energy.

Are any of these the causes of your inconsistency? If so, what response do you think God would give to you? Write out what you think God would say to you about your reason.

7. Read Judges 13—14. Although God used Samson's evil desires, how did his parents fail to restrain him (Judges 14:1-4)?

God's primary command for children is to honor their parents (Exodus 20:12; Ephesians 6:1-2). In practical terms, what do you think that means?

8. What insights into training and disciplining children do the following verses from Proverbs give?

1:8 —

3:11-12 —

3:27 —

4:11-12 —

13:24 —

19:18 —

22:6 —

22:15 —

29:15 —

29:17 —

Remember that God never condones child abuse, yet He obviously accepts physical discipline. Do you consider the "rod of discipline" (22:15) inappropriate or do you spank your child?

If you don't spank your child, why don't you?

The following seven-step process for appropriate spanking was developed by Betty Chase in her book, **Discipline Them, Love Them.**

1. Get alone with the child. Do not publicly embarrass him.
2. Ask, "What is our rule?" or "What did Mommy/Daddy say?"
3. Ask, "What did you do?"
4. Explain that you love him and equate love with correction. Say, "I love you and want to help you learn how to do the right thing the next time."
5. Spank the child in a calm manner, not in anger. Give him a few swift, but painful swats on the buttocks.
6. Comfort the child immediately after spanking him. Only the parent who spanks should do the comforting.
7. If appropriate, have the child make restitution.

Which step(s) have you left out in the spanking of your child(ren)?

Spanking should be used less frequently as a child gets older. What other methods of correction have you found effective?

9. When you take another look at Proverbs 22:6, what do you find significant about the phrase, "in the way he should go"? What responsibility does that give you as the parent?

10. What are the results of children who do and do not heed a parent's training according to these verses from Proverbs?

Do

5:1-2 —

23:15-16 —

23:24-25 —

24:13-14 —

Do Not

5:7-13 —

19:26 —

19:27 —

20:20 —

11. An important part of training our children is communicating effectively with them. What advice do these verses from Proverbs give for good communication? Apply them to your role as a mother in the form of: "A mother should..."

10:19 — *"A mother should..."*

12:18 — *"A mother should..."*

15:1-2 — *"A mother should..."*

15:23 — *"A mother should..."*

16:23-24 — *"A mother should..."*

18:13 — *"A mother should..."*

20:5 — *"A mother should..."*

25:20 — *"A mother should..."*

27:15 — *"A mother should..."*

12. Here are six disciplinary methods a mother could use: *communication* (talking about the problem); *extinction* (ignoring disobedience with the hope it will go away); *reinforcement* (reward a positive behavior with the goal it continues); *spanking*; *logical consequence* (giving an unpleasant consequence for a related disobedience); *natural consequence* (letting nature runs its course and a consequence is received without the parent getting involved).

For the following disobedient behaviors, name one or more of those methods you would recommend using from the previous list. If you indicate *reinforcement*, write out your plan for giving a reward. If you apply logical consequences, state what the consequence would be.

temper tantrum —

not picking up toys —

leaving bike out overnight —

staying out past curfew —

forgetting to brush teeth —

not doing homework —

toilet training accident —

spilling milk at meals —

not eating at meals —

talking back to parent —

deliberately hurting another child —

13. What are the most persistent disobedient behaviors your child(ren) is doing? For each one, determine which of the previously named discipline methods you'll use to respond calmly, godly, and immediately to that disobedience.

14. Write out your basic core principles about discipline: What it is meant to accomplish, why it should be consistent, how it relates to the way you love your child. If you are married, discuss this with your spouse. Then review it often and use it as your guide as you interact with your child this next week.

My Precious Princess and Daughter,

I'm sure you never imagined that becoming a mother would be so complicated. I know how tense and unsure you feel at times when you don't know how to respond to your child's disobedience. But take heart. I see your desire to rear a child who loves Me.

I can certainly understand your feelings when your child doesn't want to cooperate with your plans for his growth. After all, you just want him to learn how to make the correct choices, right? That is what I want also—for you and for all My children, but they still doubt My goodness and think I'm trying to be mean.

So don't take your child's disobedience personally. You're not a bad mother; it's just that the human nature doesn't like to be corrected. I knew giving humans the ability to make their own choices would bring trouble, but I had to do it. Otherwise, how could they choose to love Me? How could they choose to obey Me? Your children face the same consequences you do when you choose to disobey Me.

Daughter, don't give up when your son or daughter can't appreciate your efforts to teach them right from wrong. Their gratitude will come later when maturity helps them see the loving foundation you've given them. Boundaries are essential in your physical life as well as in your spiritual growth. Ask Me to be the strength you need to respond consistently to your child. I intend to bless, not harm, and I know that is your desire also. I made you a mom — and My power is sufficient in you.

Lovingly,
Your Heavenly Father, the King

10.

Releasing My Children

*R*emember when you first held your baby in your arms? You wanted to hold on forever. It's hard to envision the releasing process that must go on throughout our child's growing-up years. But letting go as they grow is as much a part of mothering as tucking them in at night. It means allowing them to take control of whatever they are capable of handling—sometimes even a tiny step before they can handle it!

1. Regardless of the age of your child, you're already taking steps in the process of letting go. How are you preparing yourself and your child for independence?

Is this easy or difficult? Why?

2. Why do you think mothers have trouble releasing their children?

Do you identify with any of those reasons?

Why would "being tied to mother's apron strings" be harmful for the child as well as the mother?

3. Read the following passages and identify the mother who released her child and what she did.

Verse(s)	_Mother_	_How she let go_
Exodus 2:1-10		
Luke 1:57-80		
Acts 16:1-4; I Timothy 1:1-3		

4. What emotions do you think these women felt as they let their sons go into unknown futures?

Why do you think they could do that?

Do you relate to any of these feelings?

Sometimes we may not be thrilled about the way God wants to use our child. Have you ever tried to prevent your child from doing something he or she felt they had to do? Why or why not? If your child is very young, can you think of any possible future situation where you might try to hold onto your child rather than let him/her go into a future you don't personally want him to explore?

5. Read Genesis 22:1-19. If you had been Sarah and knew what God had asked Abraham to do, what would you have done?

Would you obey God if He asked a similar thing of you now?

Have you ever dedicated your child(ren) to the Lord? If not, why not? If so, what did that mean to you?

Why do you think God wants us to dedicate our children to Him?

If we emotionally hold on to our children, what potential problems could result?

Have you experienced any of that?

What are you doing to encourage your children's growth, independence, and healthy separation from your immediate supervision?

6. Read John 2:1-10. In what way(s) did Mary release Jesus and yet in what way(s) did she still influence Him?

7. For each of the following groups, give one or more examples of releasing your child(ren) and yet still being a godly influence. (If your child hasn't reached a particular growth group yet, use your imagination.)

Group	_Releasing_	_Influencing_
kindergarten		
elementary school		
junior high school		
high school		
college		
career		
marriage		

What role do you think a parent should have in the life and decisions of an adult child?

8. As you remember your own growing up years, in what ways did your mother correctly release you and in what ways did she do it wrong, according to your viewpoint?

How do you feel about your mother's ability or inability to release you?

Do you recognize any ways that her ability to let go of you is now influencing your child-rearing responses? Explain by giving an example, if possible.

9. Read Luke 15:11-32. If you were the mother of that son, how would you have felt?

Would you have agreed with your husband's decision to let him go? What would you have done?

Write here what you would have said to that son before he left.

What would you have done after he left, both positively and negatively?

Is there a Bible verse you would have claimed during that time he was gone? If so, what?

Would you have agreed with that father's decision to celebrate the return of the son?

Sometimes releasing our child(ren) brings the disapproval of others in the family who may not agree with our perspective. What did the parents of the Prodigal Son experience (verses 28-30)?

How would you react to the elder son's viewpoint?

10. How can the following verses enable you to release your children as they grow up?

• Proverbs 3:5-6 —

• Proverbs 16:9 —

• Romans 5:2-5 —

• Romans 14:1-8 —

• II Peter 3:9 —

11. To what degree do you think being able to release our children depends upon us having a good relationship with God?

12. Since releasing our children requires courage and knowledge we hadn't acquired previously, what do the following verses indicate could help us?

Proverbs 27:17

Proverbs 15:22

Philippians 4:6-7

James 3:16-18

How are you depending upon one or more of those as you prepare your heart to let go of your child(ren)?

13. How can you determine what is appropriate freedom and that for which your child is not yet ready?

The next time your child presses you for more freedom, how will you respond?

My Precious Princess and Daughter,

It's frightening at times to give more freedom to your child. There are so many potential dangers that could threaten her. I see the same dangers as I free you to grow in Me. I really do understand your desire to protect her. I gave you your mother's heart of love.

But you must learn to allow her to make her own decisions. You must allow him to learn from his mistakes. That's hard. I know you'd much rather protect him from unwise choices, but, My daughter, that isn't the way I've designed life to be.

I've given each person a will and opportunities to discover My best for them. Unwise choices often draw My children closer to My loving heart in spite of—or because of—the pain they cause.

So trust My work in your child's life. Do you believe that I love her more than you? I do. Do you believe that My heart of love is greater than yours? It is.

Of course, you will set boundaries and limits; that's why I made you his parent. But don't hold on too tight. Release your grip little by little and your child won't have to try to shatter your hold all at once by rebelling against you. He doesn't want you to control his life. That's My place. I've made you his teacher, his guide, his mentor, not his master.

I promise to give you wisdom as you go along. Don't worry about the future. Just take each day as it comes and focus on the decisions you must make right now. I'll guide you day by day. I want the best for you and your child. You are the apple of My eye...and so is your child.

Lovingly,
Your Heavenly Father, the King